Guru Nanak
and
Sikhism

Ruth Nason

HODDER
Wayland

an imprint of Hodder Children's Books

Religious Lives

The Buddha and Buddhism   Krishna and Hinduism
Guru Nanak and Sikhism   Moses and Judaism
Jesus and Christianity   Muhammad and Islam

For more information on this series and other Hodder Wayland titles, go to
www.hodderwayland.co.uk

 © White-Thomson Publishing Ltd 2005

Produced for Hodder Wayland by White-Thomson Publishing Ltd
Bridgewater Business Centre, 210 High Street, Lewes, East Sussex BN7 2NH, UK

First published in 2005 by Hodder Wayland, an imprint of Hodder Children's Books

This book is adapted from *Guru Nanak and Sikhism* (*Great Religious Leaders* series) by Rajinder Singh Panesar, published by Hodder Wayland in 2002

British Library Cataloguing in Publication Data
Nason, Ruth
Guru Nanak and Sikhism. - Adapted Ed. - (Religious Lives)
1. Nanak, Guru, 1469-1538 - Juvenile literature 2. Sikhism - Juvenile literature
I.Title II.Panesar, Rajinder Singh
294.6'092
ISBN-10: 0750247916
ISBN-13: 9780750247917
Printed in China

Hodder Children's Books
A division of Hodder Headline Limited
338 Euston Road, London NW1 3BH

Title page: Sikh musicians in a gurdwara, England.

Picture Acknowledgements: The publisher would like to thank the following for permission to reproduce their pictures:
AKG 18 (Jean-Louis Nou); Art Directors and Trip Photo Library cover top, title page (H Rogers), 4 (H Rogers), 8 (H Rogers), 9 (H Rogers), 10 (H Rogers), 11 (H Rogers), 13 (H Rogers), 20 (H Rogers), 21 (H Rogers), 22 (H Rogers), 27 (H Rogers), 32–3 (H Rogers), 33 (H Rogers), 35 (Dinodia), 38 (B Dhanjal), 42 (H Rogers), 43 (H Rogers); Chapel Studios 16 (Zul Mukhida), 19 (Bipin J Mistry), 36 (Zul Mukhida); Chattar Singh Jiwan Singh 6; Circa Photo Library 5 (Bipin J Mistry), 12 (Twin Studio), 14 (John Smith), 23 (Twin Studio), 24 (Twin Studio), 25 (John Smith), 26 (John Smith), 37 (John Smith), 40, 41 (bottom) (John Smith); Eye Ubiquitous cover main (Bennett Dean), 15 (David Cumming), 28 (Bennett Dean), 29 (David Cumming), 34 (David Cumming), 39 (Tim Page); IPS Tech Corps/Inderpreet Singh 17; Christine Osborne 30; Rajinder Singh Panesar 31; Hodder Wayland 41 (top), 44, 45 (top and bottom).

Graphics and maps: Tim Mayer

Contents

1   What is Sikhism?   4

2   The Life of Guru Nanak   6

3   Guru Nanak's Teachings   14

4   The Sikh Holy Book   22

5   Sikh Holy Places   30

6   Festivals and Special Occasions   36

7   Sikhism Today   44

Glossary   46

Further Information   47

Index   48

What is Sikhism?

Sikhism is the religion of Sikh people. It started in Punjab, in the north of India, about 500 years ago. Today most Sikhs live in India, but some Sikh families have settled in other countries.

The founder of Sikhism

The religion was started by Guru Nanak. His family was Hindu, but Nanak did not like some parts of the Hindu religion. For example, Hindus worshipped many gods. Also people were divided into groups called castes, which were not allowed to mix. Some people in Punjab were Muslims. Their religion, Islam, said that all Muslims were equal. This idea of equality impressed Nanak.

He began to teach people that 'there is only one God' and 'all people are equal'.

Nanak became known as Guru Nanak. 'Guru' means 'teacher'. People who followed his teaching were 'Sikhs', which means 'learners'.

◀ This Sikh painting shows Guru Nanak praying to God.

The Gurus' teachings

After Guru Nanak, there were nine more Gurus. All the Gurus taught that Sikhs must look after their family and society. They must earn money through honest work, share food with others, meditate, and help people.

Today Sikhs learn about the Gurus' teachings from their holy book, the *Guru Granth Sahib*.

A Sikh symbol: the Khanda

The *Khanda* is a Sikh symbol. In the centre is a sword with two sharp edges. It represents the power of one God. The circle shows that God has no beginning or end. The two swords at the sides stand for worldly freedom and spiritual freedom.

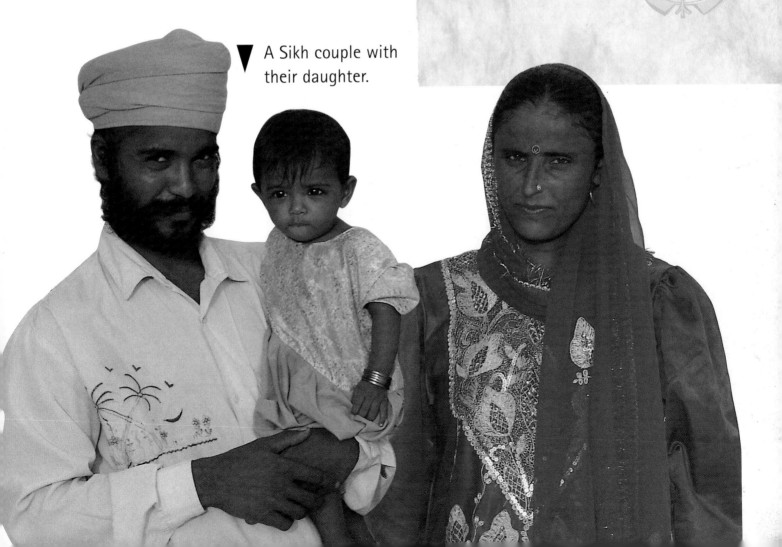

▼ A Sikh couple with their daughter.

The Life of Guru Nanak

The birth of the Guru

A man called Mheta Kalu lived in the village of Talwandi in India. One night he was in his garden, looking worried. His wife, Tripta, was about to have a baby.

Tripta's nurse came and said, 'Sir, your wife has had a son!'

'But I haven't heard a baby cry,' replied Kalu.

'I know,' said the nurse. 'He didn't cry when he was born, but smiled at me, and I saw a strange light. I think he is going to be someone special.'

Kalu said 'Thank you' to the nurse and 'Thank you God.'

▼ When Nanak was born, everyone in Talwandi came to see him.

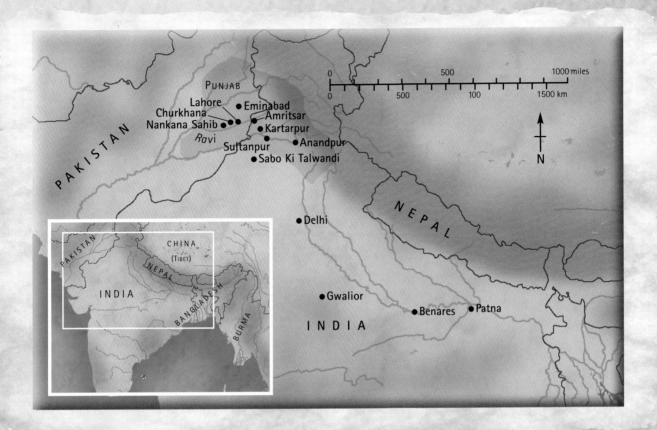

Kalu rushed indoors to Tripta. Their daughter, Nanaki, was holding her new baby brother proudly. Soon everyone in Talwandi came to congratulate the family.

A few days later an astrologer prepared a horoscope for the baby. The astrologer told Kalu, 'Sir, your son will be a great leader and many people will love and respect him.' The baby was named Nanak, which means 'unique one'.

Later, the name of Talwandi was changed to Nankana Sahib. This means 'a place where Nanak came'. It is near the city of Lahore, in present-day Pakistan.

The Guru

A Sikh called Bhai Gurdass wrote this about Guru Nanak:

The merciful God has ... sent Guru Nanak to this world. Guru established the religion and brought all four castes together. He treated prince and pauper alike ...

The Real Bargain

When Nanak grew up, Kalu was worried about how he would earn his living. Nanak liked to spend time with monks and learned people rather than doing any work.

One day Kalu gave Nanak 20 rupees and said, 'My dear son, go to the city, buy some goods and then sell them for a higher price. Good bargains like that will earn you a living.'

Nanak set off for the city with his friend Bala. On the way Nanak saw some monks under a tree. They looked weak.

Nanak asked them, 'Why are you so unhappy?'

'We have been hungry for three days.'

Nanak said to the monks, 'Please wait. I will be back.'

◀ This poster shows stories from Nanak's childhood.
Top left: At school.
Top right: A snake shades Guru Nanak from the sun.
Bottom left: Talking to a farmer.
Bottom right: Guru Nanak feeds the hungry monks.

In the city, Nanak used the 20 rupees to buy food for the monks. He took it back to them and they said, 'Oh Nanak, God will bless you and your name will shine in the world.'

Back at home, Nanak told Kalu what he had done. Kalu was cross, but Nanak asked, 'What could be a better bargain than feeding the hungry?'

Nanak's sister, Nanaki, saw that her brother and father could never get on well. She asked if Nanak could move to Sultanpur, where she and her husband lived. Kalu agreed.

In Sultanpur, Nanak became known as Guru Nanak.

Guru Nanak at Sultanpur

In Sultanpur Nanak started his first job, as a storekeeper. He also began to teach people how to love and follow God. Some called him 'Guru'.

Some time later, Guru Nanak left Sultanpur on a long journey, to take his ideas to other places in India.

▲ Guru Nanak says goodbye to the people of Sultanpur.

▲ This wall painting shows Guru Nanak's meeting with Lalo, a poor man.

Earn an honest living

Guru Nanak made four long journeys to take his teaching to more and more people. His friends, Bala and Mardana, went with him. At Eminabad, a poor man called Lalo invited them into his hut. He spread a mat on the floor and apologized for having no chairs. 'We feel comfortable on the floor,' replied the Guru. Lalo gave them some food and drink.

A rich banker named Malik Bhago also lived in Eminabad and was holding a feast. He invited Guru Nanak, but the Guru refused. Then Malik Bhago invited him again and the Guru accepted. Malik Bhago asked him rudely, 'Why go to that poor man's hut and refuse to come to my mansion?'

'I love everyone equally,' replied the Guru.

The Guru held some bread from Lalo's house in one hand and some bread from Malik Bhago's table in his other hand. Drops of milk came out of the poor man's bread. Blood oozed out of the rich man's bread.

The Guru explained to Malik Bhago:

'The poor man has earned his food by honest means, and so milk came from his humble bread. You have used harsh methods to get your food and you have treated your servants cruelly. Blood dripped from your bread because of your wickedness and greed.'

Malik Bhago understood. He changed his ways and became loved and respected by all the villagers.

Blessed and beautiful is the hut where God's praise is sung. Worthless is the palace where God is forgotten ...

Guru Granth
Sahib 745

◀ Guru Nanak squeezed the bread to show the difference between honest and dishonest ways of earning a living.

The last days of Guru Nanak

Guru Nanak's four journeys took twenty years. Then he settled by the river Ravi, in the village of Kartarpur. In the day, the people followed Guru Nanak to the fields and worked hard alongside him. In the evening they met to listen to the Guru. Everyone cooked and ate together.

A few days before he died, the Guru placed five coins and a coconut in front of one of his followers called Lehna. These were symbols of respect. The Guru said, 'From today you are the Guru of the Sikhs and I name you Angad.'

The Guru's last teaching

There is a story that Hindus and Muslims argued about what to do when Guru Nanak died.

His body was lying under a sheet. The Hindus said that Nanak was born a Hindu and so he should be cremated in the Hindu way. The Muslims said that Nanak was their holy man and so they were going to bury him as a Muslim.

A wise man appeared and listened to what they said. Then he asked, 'Have you checked what is under the sheet?'

▲ Guru Nanak told everyone that Lehna was to be the next Sikh Guru.

The ten Sikh Gurus

Each Sikh Guru chose the person who would be the Guru after him.

		Born–Died
1	Guru Nanak	1469–1539
2	Guru Angad	1504–1552
3	Guru Amar Dass	1479–1574
4	Guru Ram Dass	1534–1581
5	Guru Arjan	1563–1606
6	Guru Har Gobind	1595–1644
7	Guru Har Rai	1630–1661
8	Guru Har Krishan	1656–1664
9	Guru Tegh Bahadur	1621–1675
10	Guru Gobind Singh	1666–1708

The tenth Guru said that, after him, the teacher of the Sikhs would be their holy book, the *Guru Granth Sahib*.

▲ A poster of the ten Sikh Gurus.

They looked and found only a few flowers. The wise man had gone. They realized that it had been Guru Nanak, telling them not to quarrel. They divided the flowers and the sheet in two. The Hindus cremated their half and the Muslims buried theirs.

Guru Nanak's Teachings

Guru Nanak said that there is only one God, the creator of all. He taught Sikhs to worship only the one God. He also gave Sikhs three main rules.

▲ In this painting, a man called Puran Singh is taking someone to a Sikh hospital. This is an example of *sewa*.

Three rules

The three rules are:

1 Meditate (think about God).

2 Earn an honest living.

3 Share your earnings with needy people.

Helping others

The Guru said, 'Spend 10 per cent of your time in praying and 10 per cent of your time in doing *sewa* [voluntary work].'

Guru Nanak said that the world is like a mirror. It shows what you are like. If you are good to others, they are good to you. If you are nasty, you get nastiness back.

Life after death

The Guru believed that when a person dies, their soul does not die. It moves on to another living body or it goes to join God.

He said that we think that things are ours but, in fact, nothing really belongs to us. When we die, we even have to leave behind our body.

The five evils

The Guru taught that God judges people by what they do, and not by who they are. He taught people to avoid five evils: lust, anger, greed, attachment to possessions and self-centredness.

▼ A holy man is someone who follows the instructions of God. This Sikh holy man is holding a spear, a weapon used by Sikhs in the past.

Two types of people

Guru Nanak said that people were either *Manmukh* or *Gurmukh*.

Manmukh means a self-centred person. Their life is controlled by the five evils.

Gurmukh means someone who follows the instructions of God.

The position of women

For many years before the time of Guru Nanak, people thought that women were less important than men. Guru Nanak spoke against this idea. He taught Sikhs to call their wives *ardhangnee*, which means 'half the body'. This showed the idea that no man is complete without a woman.

The Guru asked women not to wear a veil to cover their faces. He said they should be proud to work alongside men.

All the Gurus taught that women have the right to be treated as equals to men. The wives of the Gurus helped them with their preaching.

▼ Women often lead Sikh worship. This woman is reading from the *Guru Granth Sahib*.

▲ Bhag Kaur was a brave Sikh woman who became a general and led many armies.

The courage of Bhag Kaur

Once, forty Sikhs deserted Guru Gobind Singh during a battle. A brave woman called Bhag Kaur told them that they were wrong to leave the Guru. She led them back to the battlefield and won the battle.

Guru Angad held classes for women who wanted to learn to read.

Guru Amar Dass made a law to stop women covering their faces. He also told Sikhs not to follow the custom of *sati*. When a man died and his body was cremated, it was the custom for his wife to jump on the funeral pyre and be burned with him. The Guru said that dying for no reason was wrong. He encouraged widows to marry again.

All these changes gave women an equal chance. They had the freedom to work alongside men and earn money to help to feed their family.

Everyone is equal

In the time of Guru Nanak, Muslim people called the Moguls invaded India from the north. They wanted Hindus to change to their religion. Later they conquered and ruled the land. They made all Non-Muslims pay a tax for meeting as a group or celebrating a festival.

Guru Nanak taught that all people are 'children of the one God'. Everyone is equal. He said that nobody should be treated differently because of their religion, job, colour or sex. He said that Sikhs must follow the Gurus' teachings, but also respect other religions.

▼ Sikhs have a kind of 'uniform', which shows the idea that they belong together as equals. (See page 39 for more about this.)

Langar

In Indian society people from different castes were not allowed to eat together. However, Guru Nanak held meals where everyone helped to prepare the food and all the people sat together to eat.

A meal like this was called *langar* and it became an important part of the Sikh religion. *Langar* is served in every gurdwara today, and is open to everyone. The food is always vegetarian.

► Eating *langar* at a gurdwara in Amritsar in India. A gurdwara is a Sikh place of worship.

God created all the living creatures ...
Why then should we divide
human creatures into the
high and low classes?

Guru Granth Sahib 1349

The importance of families

In India, at the time of Guru Nanak, many men went away on their own to meditate in the forests or mountains. They left their families and cut themselves off from other people and society.

Guru Nanak said that people do not need to go to the forest to find God. People must look for God inside themselves.

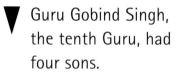

▼ Guru Gobind Singh, the tenth Guru, had four sons.

Family support

In a Sikh family one older person is in charge of the household. Everyone is respected and valued and all must work for the good of the family.

Some modern families don't all live in the same house, but they still meet regularly and stay close. Some family members may be in other countries, but often they send money to help to support the family.

▲ Guru Nanak said that people can understand the true love of God by living in a family.

Guru Nanak told Sikhs to enjoy family life and to bring up their children to know about the one God.

He said that a married person should look after their partner and bring up their children well. That would show that the person understood how God wanted people to live.

All the Sikh Gurus were married and had children, except for the eighth Guru. He died when he was only eight years old.

The Sikh Holy Book

The Sikh holy book is called the *Guru Granth Sahib.* It is a longer version of the *Adi Granth,* which was put together by Guru Arjan.

▲ This painting shows Guru Arjan blessing the Sikh people.

Guru Arjan

Guru Arjan, the fifth Sikh Guru, wanted to make one big book (a *Granth*) of all the hymns that Guru Nanak and the other Sikh Gurus had written.

First, he needed to get hold of a booklet of the Gurus' hymns, called the *Pothi.*

The Pothi

The very first *Pothi* was written by Guru Nanak. It was passed on to Guru Angad, the second Guru, who wrote another *Pothi*. Then both booklets were passed on to Guru Amar Dass, the third Guru.

Guru Amar Dass gathered all the hymns into one *Pothi* and added his own hymns too. This *Pothi* was passed to the fourth Guru, Guru Ram Dass.

When Guru Ram Dass died, the *Pothi* fell into the hands of Baba Mohan, the son of the third Guru. He would not part with it.

Guru Arjan went to Baba Mohan's house, but Baba Mohan would not let him in. So the Guru sat outside and sang a hymn. Now Baba Mohan invited him in. Guru Arjan explained that he wanted to make one book of all the Gurus' hymns and Baba Mohan gave him the *Pothi*.

The story says that Guru Arjan walked barefoot back to Amritsar, carrying the *Pothi* on his head. This showed how much he respected it.

► This painting shows Guru Arjan (below) and Guru Nanak (above). The animals in Guru Arjan's lap represent the five evils (see page 15).

This is part of the hymn that Guru Arjan sang outside Baba Mohan's house:

O Mohan, your temple is so lofty, and your mansion is unsurpassed,
O Mohan, your gates are so beautiful. They are the worship-houses of the Saints.
In these ... worship-houses, they ... sing ... the Praises of their Lord and Master.

Guru Granth Sahib 248

The Adi Granth

Guru Arjan took three years to collect the Gurus'
writings and make them into the *Adi Granth*. It was
finished in 1604.

The Guru asked his uncle, Bhai Gurdass, to help him.
There is a story that the two men sat under a big tree
in Amritsar. The Guru read out the hymns from the
Pothi and Bhai Gurdass wrote them down. They
worked slowly and carefully, to make sure that the
hymns were written clearly and accurately.

The hymns of the fourth Guru and of Guru Arjan
himself were also written down. Finally, Guru Arjan
chose some hymns by fifteen other holy men and
these were written in the *Adi Granth* too. The fifteen
other holy men were not all Sikhs, but their hymns
fitted with the teachings of Guru Nanak.

◄ This painting shows
Guru Arjan reading
the *Adi Granth*. The
man behind him is
waving a fan made
from peacock feathers,
to show respect.

A book for everyone

Some hymns in the *Adi Granth* were written by men who were considered quite low in society. Some were written by Muslim holy men. By putting hymns by these people with the hymns of the Gurus, Guru Arjan wanted to show that God sees everyone as equal. The Guru wanted the *Adi Granth* to be for all people.

When the writing was finished, the pages were sent to the city of Lahore, to be bound in a hard cover.

The Sikhs now had one book of the Gurus' writings, which they knew was genuine.

▲ This copy of the Sikh holy book, at Amritsar, was handwritten about 200 years ago.

Harmandir Sahib

Guru Arjan built a beautiful Sikh place of worship in Amritsar. It was built in the middle of a lake, with just one bridge leading to it. The Guru named the holy place *Harmandir Sahib*, which means 'divine house of God'. Today it is also known as the Golden Temple.

Guru Arjan was happy that, through his work, the Sikh religion now had its own holy place and its own holy book, the *Adi Granth*.

On 30 August 1604, the *Adi Granth* was taken to the main hall at *Harmandir Sahib*. Everyone bowed to it and sat on the floor, to show respect.

▼ This is the most important room of *Harmandir Sahib*, where the *Adi Granth* was placed in 1604.

The most important place

In the main hall the *Adi Granth* was placed on a low platform with a canopy above it. The holy book was covered with a beautiful cloth called a *rumalla*. A fan called a *chauri* was waved over it to show respect.

Another room was prepared where the *Adi Granth* would be kept overnight. In the morning it was carried into the main hall again.

Gurdwaras

A gurdwara is a place where Sikhs go to worship. There are gurdwaras all around the world today. In all of them the Sikh holy book rests on a platform with a canopy. People sit on the floor, facing the holy book. There is also a special room to keep the holy book overnight.

◄ These Sikhs at *Harmandir Sahib* are carrying the holy book to the room where it is kept overnight.

Guru Gobind Singh

The *Adi Granth* was compiled by the fifth Sikh Guru, Guru Arjan. A hundred years later, in 1706, the tenth Guru, Guru Gobind Singh, revised it by adding the hymns of the ninth Guru, Guru Tegh Bahadur.

Guru Gobind Singh said that, after he died, Sikhs should follow the holy book as their Guru. He renamed the *Adi Granth* as the *Guru Granth Sahib*.

The Guru Granth Sahib

Today many Sikhs visit the gurdwara twice a day to pay respect to the *Guru Granth Sahib*.

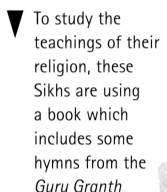

▼ To study the teachings of their religion, these Sikhs are using a book which includes some hymns from the *Guru Granth Sahib*.

Special readings

The *Guru Granth Sahib* has 1,430 pages. On special occasions, it is read out all the way through, without stopping. Five volunteers take turns to read for two hours each. The whole reading takes 48 hours. The name for this non-stop reading is *Akhand Path*.

▲ This man is taking part in an *Akhand Path*. He holds a fan called a *chauri* to show respect for the *Guru Granth Sahib*.

The person at the gurdwara who reads from the *Guru Granth Sahib* is called the *Granthi*. He or she opens the book at random and reads out the first part of the left-hand page. This is called an 'order of the Guru' or a 'guidance of the Guru'. It helps Sikhs to know what is the right thing to do.

Dasam Granth

Guru Gobind Singh wrote many hymns but he did not add any of them to the *Guru Granth Sahib*. The hymns of Guru Gobind Singh are written down in another book, called the *Dasam Granth*. This means the 'book of the tenth Guru'.

Sikh Holy Places

Sikhs built gurdwaras in places that were important in the lives of the Gurus.

Gurdwara Janamasthan

Gurdwara Janamasthan marks the birthplace of Guru Nanak, in the village now called Nankana Sahib (see page 7).

Many Sikhs visit this gurdwara on Guru Nanak's birthday. It has 300 rooms for visitors to stay overnight.

▲ Gurdwara Janamasthan was built to mark the place where Guru Nanak was born.

Gurdwara Patti Sahib

This gurdwara is also in Nankana Sahib. It was built to mark the place where Guru Nanak went to school. The Guru learned the Sanskrit, Arabic and Persian languages. He also wrote a hymn called *Patti* at this place.

Gurdwara Sacha Sauda and Gurdwara Janamasthan (page 30) were both built by the Emperor Ranjit Singh in the nineteenth century.

Gurdwara Sacha Sauda

Gurdwara Sacha Sauda was built where Guru Nanak fed the hungry monks (see pages 8-9). The gurdwara has many rooms for visitors to stay the night. Four times a year Sikhs hold an *Akhand Path* (see page 29) at this gurdwara.

Gurdwara Kartar Pur Sahib

Gurdwara Kartar Pur Sahib was built by the river Ravi in Kartarpur, where Guru Nanak died (see page 12). It is hard to keep this gurdwara in good condition because it is by the river and surrounded by forest, but it has been repaired in recent years.

Harmandir Sahib

The most important gurdwara for Sikhs is *Harmandir Sahib* in the town of Amritsar. It was founded in 1588 by Guru Arjan (see page 26).

Two hundred years later, in 1803, Emperor Ranjit Singh arranged for the dome and roof to be covered with gold leaf. The gurdwara then became known as the Golden Temple.

Sikhs try to visit the Golden Temple at least once in their lifetime.

Akal Takhat

▼ The Golden Temple stands in the middle of an artificial lake. It is part of a complex of many Sikh buildings.

The *Akal Takhat* is an important building which stands opposite *Harmandir Sahib*. It was built in 1609 by Guru Har Gobind, the sixth Guru. Rules for the Sikh people are decided at the *Akal Takhat* and sent out from there.

Gurdwara Sis Ganj

Gurdwara Sis Ganj is in Delhi, the capital of India. It was built where the ninth Guru, Guru Tegh Bahadur, died. He was beheaded because he spoke against a Mogul emperor who was forcing all people to become Muslims.

Gurdwara Bangla Sahib

Gurdwara Bangla Sahib is also in Delhi. It was built where the eighth Guru, Guru Har Krishan, looked after people who were ill with smallpox. He himself died of smallpox when he was eight years old.

▲ Gurdwara Bangla Sahib in Delhi.

As well as the *Akal Takhat* (see page 32), there are four other gurdwaras where Sikh rules are decided. They are called *Takhat*, which means 'seat of authority'. These four gurdwaras mark events in the life of Guru Gobind Singh, the tenth Guru.

▲ In the main hall of Takhat Sri Patna Sahib, there are three copies of the *Guru Granth Sahib*.

Takhat Sri Patna Sahib

Takhat Sri Patna Sahib is in the city of Patna in India. It marks the birthplace of the Guru.

Takhat Sri Kesgarh Sahib

This gurdwara is in Anandpur. It marks the place where Guru Gobind Singh founded the *Khalsa* (see page 39). It is the second place that Sikhs try to visit at least once in their lifetime, after *Harmandir Sahib* (see page 32).

Takhat Sri Dam Dama Sahib

This gurdwara is in the village of Sabo Ki Talwandi. Guru Gobind Singh rested there for almost a year, on his way to the south of India. It was there that the Guru revised the *Adi Granth* in 1706 (see page 28).

Takhat Sri Hazur Sahib

This gurdwara is in Nanded, India, where Guru Gobind Singh died in 1708. It was there that the Guru gave the *Adi Granth* its new name, the *Guru Granth Sahib* (see page 28). He told Sikhs that, after his death, the *Guru Granth Sahib* would be their teacher.

▼ Takhat Sri Dam Dama Sahib was built by Emperor Ranjit Singh.

Festivals and Special Occasions

Many Sikh festivals celebrate events in the lives of the Gurus. This type of festival is called a *Gurpurb*.

The main Gurpurbs

The main *Gurpurbs* are Guru Nanak's birthday, Guru Gobind Singh's birthday, Guru Arjan's martyrdom, Guru Tegh Bahadur's martyrdom and the day when the *Adi Granth* was placed in *Harmandir Sahib* (see page 26).

What happens on a Gurpurb?

Sikhs celebrate each festival at the gurdwara. The celebrations are usually on the day of the *Gurpurb*, but sometimes on the weekend afterwards.

▼ Many Sikhs take part in preparing the meal that is shared at the gurdwara. These women are making chapattis.

A reading of the whole of the *Guru Granth Sahib* is started (see page 29) so that it ends on the *Gurpurb*. Sikhs go to the gurdwara to listen to the reading. They also sing hymns and say prayers. Their preachers tell the story of the festival. Then everyone shares the meal called *langar*.

Sometimes there is a procession through the town. The *Guru Granth Sahib* is carried at the front of the procession. The people follow, singing hymns.

▲ In Anandpur in India a procession takes place on Guru Nanak's birthday.

At home

At home, on a *Gurpurb*, Sikhs get up early, have a bath and put on new colourful clothes. Some families exchange gifts and visit other family members or friends. There may be a special feast.

Dates of the Gurpurbs

Guru Nanak's birthday: October or November.
Guru Gobind Singh's birthday: December or January.
Adi Granth day: August or September.
Guru Arjan's martyrdom: June.
Guru Tegh Bahadur's martyrdom: November.

The dates change from year to year because the Sikh calendar is different from the Western calendar. It is based on cycles of the moon, not the sun.

▲ These people are celebrating the *Baisakhi* spring festival with a parade and music and dancing.

Baisakhi

The *Baisakhi* festival takes place in April on the Western calendar. It is a spring festival in northwest India. It existed before the Sikh religion began.

For Sikhs everywhere, *Baisakhi* has an extra meaning. It was at the time of *Baisakhi* in 1699 that Guru Gobind Singh, the tenth Guru, started the *Khalsa*, the community of Sikhs. He gave Sikhs five things to wear, to show they belong to the *Khalsa*. They are known as the 'five Ks'.

A special thing that Sikhs do at the *Baisakhi* festival is renew the flag which flies outside their gurdwara.

Divali

The Sikh *Divali* festival takes place in October or November. Sikhs remember the sixth Guru, Guru Har Gobind. He was kept in jail because he would not pay the tax that the Mogul rulers made non-Muslims pay (see page 18). When he was set free, he went to Amritsar and Sikhs lit up *Harmandir Sahib* (see page 32) to celebrate.

At the *Divali* festival today Sikhs decorate their gurdwaras and homes with lights and candles.

▼ There is a ceremony for joining the *Khalsa*. The person is given a liquid called *amrit*, made from sugar and water.

The Khalsa

In 1699 Sikhs in India were being persecuted. Guru Gobind Singh wanted them to be strong and stand up for their religion. He asked them to join together to make the *Khalsa*. He said that members of the *Khalsa* must wear the 'five Ks' to show that they are Sikhs. The five Ks are: *kesh* (uncut hair), *kangha* (wooden comb), *kara* (steel bracelet), *kirpan* (sword) and *kachera* (undershorts). Sikhs today still become members of the *Khalsa* and wear the five Ks.

This family took their baby to the gurdwara for a naming ceremony.

A new baby

When a baby is born, Sikhs may whisper the word '*Waheguru*' into the baby's ear. This is a name that Sikhs use for God. It means 'wonderful Lord'.

Naming the baby

The family takes the new baby to the gurdwara and some prayers are said.

Then the *Granthi* (reader) opens the *Guru Granth Sahib* and tells the family what is the first letter on the page. They choose a name for the baby beginning with that letter.

Sikh names

The same first name (e.g. Pritam) can be for a boy or a girl.
All males have the second name Singh ('lion'). All females have the second name Kaur ('princess'). The surname (e.g. Panesar) comes next. So a boy would be Pritam Singh Panesar, and a girl would be Pritam Kaur Panesar.

The wedding ceremony

An important part of a Sikh wedding ceremony is the reading of the *Lavan*, a hymn by Guru Ram Dass, the fourth Guru. The hymn has four verses.

After each verse is read, the bride and the groom walk once around the *Guru Granth Sahib* and then bow to it. The groom leads, holding one end of a long scarf. The bride follows, holding the other end. The scarf is a symbol of the soft but strong bond between a husband and a wife.

► Marriage and family life are important to Sikhs.

▼ At their wedding, the bride and groom bow in front of the *Guru Granth Sahib*.

Death

Guru Nanak said that death is a normal part of
our life cycle. Therefore there is no reason to be
afraid of death. One part of the *Guru Granth Sahib*
says: 'Death ... brings joy to me because, by dying,
I can merge with God.'

Funerals in Western countries

When a Sikh dies, a hymn called *Kirtan Sohila* is
recited. In Western countries the body is then
taken away by a funeral director and a date for
the funeral is decided.

▼ On the day of a funeral
the body is taken in a
coffin to the family's
home. People say their
last goodbye.

On the day of the funeral the body is washed, clothed and brought home so that all the family can see their loved one for the last time. Some hymns are sung.

The body may also be taken to the gurdwara so that friends can pay their respects. More hymns are sung.

Then the body is taken to a crematorium, to be burned. The *Kirtan Sohila* is sung again and the last prayers are said.

In India

In India, the cremation takes place immediately after someone dies.

Life after death

Sikhs believe that, when a person dies, their soul passes into another body (see page 15). This can be the body of any living thing. However, from a human body, it is possible for the soul to be united with God. Sikhs believe that this will happen if a person lives their life in the way that God wishes.

▶ These people are saying prayers at the gurdwara before the body is taken away for cremation.

Sikhism Today

Guru Nanak began the Sikh religion in India, just over 500 years ago. Today Sikhs live all over the world.

The Sikh homeland

Sikhism began in Punjab. This is their homeland and the largest number of Sikhs in the world still live there.

Punjab today is one of the richest parts of India. Sikhs have adapted well to modern technology and many are successful people.

Around the world

Many Sikhs have moved away from Punjab to other countries. In many places they have gained respect as friendly and hard-working people. Even so, Sikhs have also faced discrimination.

▲ This Sikh family lives in New York, USA. Both the woman and her husband wear turbans.

Uncut hair

Sikhs' clothing makes them stand out. Most Sikhs follow the rule that Guru Gobind Singh gave them, never to cut their hair. Men wear a turban to keep their long hair neat. However, some Sikh people do not keep this rule. They cut their hair and men are clean-shaven.

Challenges today

In the past, Sikhs were persecuted. The Gurus taught them to be strong and brave against the people who persecuted them. Some Sikhs say that there is a new struggle today. They must be strong and stand up for Sikh beliefs in the face of harmful influences such as fashion, the media and drugs. They have set up many organizations to teach young Sikhs the values of Sikhism.

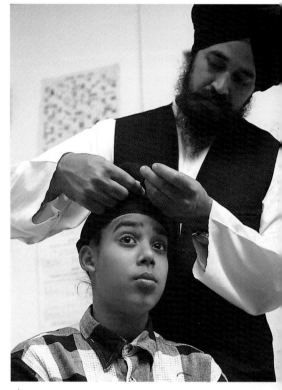

▲ A father helps his son to cover his long hair with a headdress called a *patka*.

► Life is very different in the UK today from in Punjab 500 years ago. Yet Guru Nanak's ideas, for example about equality, are still very relevant.

Glossary

astrologer   someone who studies the positions of stars and planets, and explains in a horoscope how this could influence a person's life.

bless   to wish happiness on someone.

castes   social classes in Hindu society.

ceremony   a fixed, formal way of celebrating an event such as a marriage or the time when someone joins a religion or an organization.

cremate   to burn a dead body.

crematorium   a place for cremating bodies.

five Ks   five things that Sikhs wear to show that they belong to the religion. In the Punjabi language, the word for each thing begins with a 'k'. One is *kesh*: uncut hair.

funeral pyre   a heap of material which will burn, for a body to be cremated.

Granthi   someone who reads the *Guru Granth Sahib* at the gurdwara, when Sikhs gather to worship there.

gurdwara   a Sikh place of worship. It can be any place where a copy of the *Guru Granth Sahib* is kept. Every gurdwara building has the orange Sikh flag outside it.

Guru   teacher.

Guru Granth Sahib   the Sikh holy book.

Harmandir Sahib   the most important Sikh holy place, in Amritsar. It is also known as the Golden Temple.

holy   kept separate and special, for God.

hymn   a song praising God.

Khalsa   the community of Sikhs around the world.

langar   a meal that everyone shares after worshipping together in the gurdwara.

martyrdom   the death of someone who is killed as a result of holding on to their beliefs.

meditate   to think about God.

merciful   willing to forgive.

Moguls   Muslim people who originally came from Mongolia. They ruled much of India from the sixteenth to the nineteenth century.

monk   a man who lives as part of a religious community, with its own rules.

Muslims   people who follow the religion called Islam.

patka   a head covering worn by Sikh boys.

pauper   a very poor person.

persecute   to deliberately find and cause suffering to people because of their beliefs or the group they belong to.

rupee   an Indian coin.

sewa   'service', helping other people.

soul   spiritual part of a person, which some people believe lives on after the body dies.

turban   a long strip of cloth which Sikh men tie around their head to cover their long hair.

Further Information

Books to read

My Sikh Year (*Year of Religious Festivals* series) by Cath Senker (Hodder Wayland, 2003)

Sikh Gurdwara (*Where We Worship* series) by Kanwaljit Kaur-Singh (Franklin Watts, 2005)

Sikh Stories (*Storyteller* series) by Anita Ganeri and Rachel Phillips (Evans Publishing, 2000)

The Guru's Family: a story about Guru Nanak's birthday (*Celebration Stories* series) by Pratima Mitchell (Hodder Wayland, 2002)

Visiting a Gurdwara (*Start-Up Religion* series) by Kanwaljit Kaur-Singh and Ruth Nason (Evans Publishing, 2005)

Places to visit

Many gurdwaras welcome groups of visitors who wish to learn about Sikhism and see the Sikh place of worship. Visitors should take off their shoes and wear something to cover their heads when they go into the main prayer hall where the *Guru Granth Sahib* is kept.

Resources for teachers

http://www.reonline.org.uk
A 'family of websites' including some for teachers and some for pupils. Serves as a gateway to over 300 RE resources drawn from all over the web.

http://re-xs.ucsm.ac.uk
RE Exchange Service (linked to National Grid for Learning) with a 'Teachers' Cupboard' resource page.

http://www.theredirectory.org.uk

http://sikhs.org

http://bbc.co.uk/religion/religions/sikhism

http://www.sikhnet.com

http://allaboutsikhs.com/home.php

BBC Education produces schools media resources on different faiths. See: http://www.bbc.co.uk/schools

Channel 4 produces schools media resources on different faiths, including *Animated World Faiths*. Download catalogue from: http://www.channel4.com/learning

The Institute for Indian Art and Culture
The Bhavan Centre, 4a Castletown Road, West Kensington, London W14 9HQ
Tel: 0207 381 3086   http://www.bhavan.net

The Sikh Missionary Society
10 Featherstone Road, Southall, Middx UB2 5AA
Tel: 0208 574 1902   Fax: 0208 8574 1912

DTF (the book and artefact shop)
117 Soho Road, Handsworth, Birmingham B21
Tel: 0121 515 1183

Index

Adi Granth 22-28, 35, 36, 37
Akal Takhat 32, 34
Akhand Path 29, 31
amrit 39
Amritsar 7, 19, 23, 24, 25, 26, 32, 39
Anandpur 7, 34, 37
astrologer 7

babies 40
Baisakhi 38
Bala 8, 10
'bargain, real' 8-9
Bhag Kaur 17
Bhai Gurdass 7, 24

calendar 37
castes 4, 7, 19
chauri 27, 29

Dasam Granth 29
death 15, 42–43
Divali 39

Eminabad 7, 10
equality 4, 18, 25, 45

families 20-21, 37, 41
five evils 15, 23
five Ks 38, 39
funerals 42–43

God, one 4, 5, 14, 18, 21

Golden Temple 26, 32 (see also *Harmandir Sahib*)
Granthi 29, 40
gurdwaras 19, 27, 30-35, 36, 37, 39, 40, 43
Gurpurbs 36–37
Guru Amar Dass 13, 17, 22
Guru Angad 12, 13, 17, 22
Guru Arjan 13, 22-28, 32, 36, 37
Guru Gobind Singh 13, 17, 20, 28, 29, 34, 35, 38, 39, 45
Guru Granth Sahib 5, 13, 16, 22, 28, 29, 35, 37, 40, 41, 42
Guru Har Gobind 13, 32, 39
Guru Har Krishan 13, 33
Guru Nanak 4, 22, 23, 24, 30, 31, 42, 44, 45
 birthday 30, 36, 37
 life 6-13
 teachings 14-21
Guru Ram Dass 13, 22, 23, 41
Gurus, Sikh 5, 13, 16, 21
Guru Tegh Bahadur 13, 28, 33, 36, 37

hair 39, 45
Harmandir Sahib 26, 27, 32, 34, 39
Hindus 4, 12, 13
holy book 5, 13, 22-29 (see also *Guru Granth Sahib*)
holy man 15

Kartarpur 7, 12, 31
Khalsa 34, 38, 39
khanda symbol 5

Lalo 10-11
langar 19, 37

Malik Bhago 10–11
Mardana 10
marriage 21, 41
Moguls 18, 33, 39
monks, hungry 8-9, 31
Muslims 4, 12, 13, 18, 25

names 40
Nankana Sahib 7, 30

Punjab 4, 7, 44, 45
Puran Singh 14

Ranjit Singh, Emperor 31, 32, 35
rules, Sikh 14, 32, 34, 45

sewa 14
soul 15, 43
Sultanpur 7, 9

Takhat 34
Talwandi 6, 7
turbans 44, 45

wedding ceremony 41
women in Sikhism 16-17